The Impressionists

Alfred Sisley (1839-1899) *The Flood at Port-Marly*

Grange BOOKS

Berthe Morisot (1841-1895) *Julie Manet and her Nurse*

The Impressionists

Compiled By Anna Nicholas

Gustave Loiseau (1865-1935) *Cliffs in Normandy*

A selection of poems and quotations

The Publishers would like to acknowledge the following for
permission to reproduce copyright material:
Pages 9 and 10, Adrian Henri and Rogers Coleridge White for
'Garden: Giverny' and 'Four Studies of Dieppe for the Painter
Nicholas Horsfield' by Adrian Henri; Page 16, Faber & Faber
for 'Daybreak' by Stephen Spender; Page 46, The Society of
Authors, representatives for the estate of Walter de la Mare for
'Six Centuries Now Have Gone' by Walter de la Mare.

The Publishers have made every effort to trace copyright
holders of material reproduced within this compilation. If,
however, they have inadvertantly made any error they would
be grateful for notification.

Many thanks to Paperchase, London for kindly allowing us to
use their papers.

Pictures courtesy of The Bridgeman Art Library.

Pictures courtesy of The Bridgeman Art Library

Published in 1994 by Grange Books
An imprint of Grange Books PLC
The Grange, Grange Yard
London SE1 3AG

Copyright © 1995 Regency House Publishing Limited

ISBN 1 85627 695 3

Printed in Italy

Pierre Auguste Renoir (1841-1919) *Female Nude on a Couch*

Pierre Auguste Renoir (1841-1919) *Place de la Trinité*

six

'The shifting shimmer of gleam and shadow

which the changing reflected lights,

themselves influenced by every

neighbouring thing, cast upon each advancing and

departing figure, and the fleeting combinations in

which these dissimilar reflections form one harmony or

many, such are the favourite effects of Renoir – nor

can we wonder that this infinite complexity of

execution induces him to seek more hazardous success

in things widely opposed to nature.'

Stéphane Mallarmé 1842-1898

'*I have a horror of the word "flesh" which has become so overused... What I love is skin: a young girl's skin that is pink, and shows that she has a good circulation. But above all else I love serenity.*'

Pierre Auguste Renoir 1841-1919

Pierre August Renoir *Baigneuse*

eight

*Delphiniums, sweet williams,
purple gladioli,
against yellow asters, marigolds,
the whirl of sunflowers;
glimpsed pink walls against emerald shutters.*

*A bamboo-grove
lurks in the shadows by the lily-pond,
patient as a tiger.
Lovers kiss on a Japanese bridge
watched by the bearded phantom
from behind the willows,
sad as a blind girl in a summer garden.*

Garden, Giverny. Adrian Henri

Claude Monet (1840-1926) *Waterlily Pond*

one

light arrives in the harbour
like a monarch at a painter's door
the brush poised to trap
like a lobsterpot.

two

apple-orchards moult pink into summer
an excitement of melon against green lawns
the haze of sardines grilling
hydrangeas pushing in at the night window.

three

paint glitters like mackerel spilt on the quayside
the breath of ferries and fishingboats
caught against an impasto of cliffs
framed in an oval sunset.

four

burnt sienna scumbled against zinc white
where only the green-capped stones, gaunt as
Frankenstein,
remember the suck of boots,
the crunch of landingcraft.

Four Studies of Dieppe
For the painter Nicholas Horsfield.

Adrian Henri

François Flameng (1856-1923) *Elegante au Bord de la Mer*

'Cézanne's landscapes...grandiose and yet so painted, so supple. Why? Sensation is there.'
Camille Pissarro 1831-1903

Paul Cézanne (1838-1906) *Mont Sainte-Victoire*

e l e v e n

'Morisot seems to paint with her nerves on edge, providing a few scanty traces to create complete, disquieting evocations.'

Octave Mirbeau

Edgar Degas (1834-1917) *Woman Combing her Hair*

*'I take all the colour out of
(my pastels) that I can, by putting them in the
sun'*

'But what do you use, then, to get colours
of such brightness?'

'Opaque colour, Monsieur.'

Edgar Degas to Ambroise Vollard

twelve

Berthe Morisot (1841-1895) *Dans un Parc*

thirteen

Earth has not anything to show more fair:

Dull would he be of soul who could pass by

A sight so touching in its majesty:

This City now doth like a garment wear

The beauty of the morning; silent, bare,

Ships, towers, domes, theatres, and temples lie

Open unto the fields, and to the sky;

All bright and glittering in the smokeless air.

Never did sun more beautifully steep

In his first splendour valley, rock, or hill;

Ne'er saw I, never felt, a calm so deep!

The river glideth at his own sweet will:

Dear God! the very houses seem asleep;

And all that mighty heart is lying still!

Upon Westminster Bridge. William Wordsworth 1770-1850

Claude Monet (1840-1926) *The Thames Below Westminster*

fifteen

At dawn she lay with her profile at that angle

Which, when she sleeps, seems the carved face of an angel.

Her hair a harp, the hand of a breeze follows

And plays, against the white cloud of the pillows.

Then, in a flush of rose, she woke, and her eyes that opened

Swam in blue through her rose flesh that dawned.

From her dew of lips, the drop of one word

Fell like the first of fountains: murmured

'Darling', upon my ears the song of the first bird.

'My dream becomes my dream,' she said, 'come true,

I waken from you to my dream of you.'

Oh, my own wakened dream that dared assume

The audacity of her sleep. Our dreams

Poured into each other's arms, like streams.

Stephen Spender b.1909

Lilian Westcott Hale (1881-1963) *Zeffy in Bed*

Fair pledges of a fruitful tree,
    Why do ye fall so fast?
    Your date is not so past,
But you may stay yet here awhile
    To blush and gently smile,
        And go at last.

What, were ye born to be
    An hour or half's delight,
    And so to bid good-night?
'Twas pity Nature brought ye forth
    Merely to show your worth,
        And lose you quite.

But you are lovely leaves, where we
    May read how soon things have
    Their end, though ne'er so brave:
And after they have shown their pride
    Like you, awhile they glide
        Into the grave.

Ernest Quost (1844-1931) *Apple Trees in Flower*

Robert Herrick 1591-1674

s e v e n t e e n

'One enjoyed the day, the fatigue, the speed, the free and vibrant out-of-doors, the glittering of the water, the sun flashing over the earth, the shimmering flame of all that dazes and dazzles in the sauntering outings, that almost animal intoxication with life conveyed by a great streaming river, blinded by light and fine weather.'

From: *Manette Salomon*. E & J de Goncourt

Claude Monet (1840-1926) *La Grenouillère*

Beneath is spread like a green sea
The waveless plain of Lombardy,
Bounded by the vaporous air,
Islanded by cities fair;
Underneath day's azure eyes,
Ocean's nursling, Venice lies, –
A peopled labyrinth of walls,
Amphitrite's destined halls,
Which her hoary sire now paves
With his blue and beaming waves.
Lo! the sun upsprings behind,
Broad, red, radiant, half-reclined
On the level quivering line
Of the waters crystalline;
And before that chasm of light,
As within a furnace bright,
Column, tower, and dome, and spire,
Shine like obelisks of fire,
Pointing with inconstant motion
From the altar of dark ocean
To the sapphire-tinted skies;
As the flames of sacrifice
From the marble shrines did rise
As to pierce the dome of gold
Where Apollo spoke of old.

From: *Written Among the Euganean Hills, North Italy.*
William Wordsworth 1770-1850

Joseph Mallord William Turner (1775-1851) *Venice: The Bridge of Sighs*

Claude Monet (1840-1926) *The Rocks of Belle-Ile*

Here, in this little Bay,
Full of tumultuous life and great repose,
Where, twice a day,
The purposeless, glad ocean comes and goes,
Under high cliffs, and far from the huge town,
I sit me down.
For want of me the world's course will not fail;
When all its work is done, the lie shall rot;
The truth is great, and shall prevail,
When none cares whether it prevail or not.

t w e n t y

Coventry Patmore 1823-1896

twenty-one   Eva Gonzales (1849-1883) *Henri Guérard Relaxing on the Beach*

See what a mass of gems the city wears

Upon her broad live bosom! row on row

Rubies and emeralds and amethysts glow.

See! that huge circle, like a necklace, stares

With thousands of bold eyes to heaven, and dares

The golden stars to dim the lamps below.

And in the mirror of the mire I know

The moon has left her image unawares.

That's the great town at night: I see her breasts,

Prick'd out with lamps they stand like huge black towers,

I think they move! I hear her panting breath.

And that's her head where the tiara rests.

And in her brain, through-lanes as dark as death,

Men creep like thoughts ... The lamps are like pale flowers.

Impression de Nuit: London. Lord Alfred Douglas b. 1870

James Abbott McNeill Whistler (1834-1903)
Nocturne, Blue and Gold: Old Battersea Bridge

twenty-two

On a starred night Prince Lucifer uprose,

Tired of his dark dominion swung the fiend

Above the rolling ball in cloud part screened,

Where sinners hugged their spectre of repose,

Poor prey to his hot fit of pride were those.

And now upon his western wing he leaned,

Now his huge bulk o'er Afric's sands careened,

Now the black planet shadowed Arctic snows.

Soaring through wider zones that pricked his scars

With memory of the old revolt from Awe,

He reached a middle height, and at the stars,

Which are the brain of heaven, he looked, and sank.

Around the ancient track marched rank on rank

The army of unalterable law.

Lucifer by Starlight. George Meredith 1828-1909

Vincent van Gogh (1853-1890) *The Starry Night*

t w e n t y - t h r e e

In a coign of the cliff between lowland and highland,
 At the sea-down's edge between windward and lee,
Walled round with rocks as an inland island,
 The ghost of a garden fronts the sea.
A girdle of brushwood and thorn encloses
 The steep square slope of the blossomless bed
Where the weeds that grew green from the graves of its roses
        Now lie dead.

The fields fall southwards, abrupt and broken,
 To the low last edge of the long lone land.
If a step should sound or a word be spoken,
 Would a ghost not rise at the strange guest's hand?
So long have the grey bare walks lain guestless,
 Through branches and briars if a man make way,
He shall find no life but the sea-wind's, restless
        Night and day.

From: *A Forsaken Garden*. Algernon Charles Swinburne 1837-1909

Claude Monet (1814-1926) *Fisherman's Cottage on the Cliffs at Varengeville*

twenty-five

Every branch big with it,
  Bent every twig with it;
Every fork like a white web-foot;
Every street and pavement mute:
Some flakes have lost their way, and grope back upward, when
Meeting those meandering down they turn and descend again.
  The palings are glued together like a wall,
  And there is no waft of wind with the fleecy fall.

    A sparrow enters the tree,
    Whereupon immediately
  A snow-lump thrice his own slight size
  Descends on him and showers his head and eyes,
      And overturns him
      And near inurns him,
    And lights on a nether twig, when its brush
Starts off a volley of other lodging lumps with a rush.

    The steps are a blanched slope,
    Up which, with feeble hope,
  A black cat comes, wide-eyed and thin:
      And we take him in.

Snow in the Suburbs. Joachin Miller 1837-1913

Eugéne Chigot (1860-1923) *The Garden Under Snow*

twenty-seven

I think that I shall never see
A poem lovely as a tree.

A tree whose hungry mouth is prest
Against the earth's sweet flowing breast;

A tree that looks at God all day,
And lifts her leafy arms to pray;

A tree that may in summer wear
A nest of robins in her hair;

Upon whose bosom snow has lain;
Who intimately lives with rain.

Poems are made by fools like me,
But only God can make a tree.

Joyce Kilmer 1886-1918

Alfred Sisley (1839-1899) *The Loing Canal*

Paul Cézanne (1838-1906) *Landscape with Viaduct: Mont Sainte-Victoire*

O, for a draught of vintage, that hath been

  Cool'd a long age in the deep-delvèd earth,

Tasting of Flora and the country green,

  Dance, and Provençal song, and sun-burnt mirth:

O for a beaker full of the warm South,

  Full of the true, the blushful Hippocrene,

    With beaded bubbles winking at the brim,

      And purple-stainèd mouth;

That I might drink, and leave the world unseen,

  And with thee fade away into the forest dim:

From: *Ode to a Nightingale*. John Keats 1795-1821

Pierre Auguste Renoir (1841-1919) *Odalisque: Woman of Algiers*

How splendid in the morning glows
   the lily; with what grace he throws
His supplication to the rose:
   do roses nod the head, Yasmin?
But when the silver dove descends
   I find the little flower of friends
Whose very name that sweetly ends
   I say when I have said 'Yasmin'.

The morning light is clear and cold,
   I dare not in the night behold
A deeper light, a deeper gold
   a glory too far shed, Yasmin.
But when the deep red eye of day
   is level with the lone highway,
And some to Mecca turn to pray,
   and I toward thy bed, Yasmin,

Or when the wind beneath the moon
   is drifting like a soul aswoon,
And harping planets talk love's tune
   with milky wings outspread, Yasmin,
Shower down thy love, O burning bright!
   for one night or the other night
Will come the Gardener in white,
   and gathered flowers are dead, Yasmin!

Hassan's Serenade. James Elroy Flecker 1884-1915

Beauty sat bathing by a spring,
  Where fairest shades did hide her;
The winds blew calm, the birds did sing,
  The cool streams ran beside her.
My wanton thoughts enticed mine eye
To see what was forbidden:
But better memory said Fie;
  So vain desire was chidden -
    Hey nonny nonny O!
    Hey nonny nonny!

Into a slumber then I fell,
  And fond imagination
Seemed to see, but could not tell,
  Her feature or her fashion:
And ev'n as babes in dreams do smile,
  And sometimes fall a-weeping,
So I awaked as wise that while
  As when I fell a-sleeping.

Anthony Munday 1553-1633

Pierre Auguste Renoir (1841-1919) *The Blond Bather*

'... the circular promenade where...a group of women awaited arrivals at one or another of the three bars behind which, heavily made-up and wilting, three vendors of refreshment and love held court.'

Guy de Maupassant in *Bel Ami* speaking of the Folies-Bergère

Edouard Manet (1832-1882) *The Bar at the Folies-Bergère*

t h i r t y - t h r e e

'... shows the arrival of a train in full sunlight. It is a joyous, lively canvas. People hurriedly get down from their cars, smoke puffs off into the background and rises upward, and the sunlight, passing through the windows, gilds the gravel of the tracks as well as the trains. In some paintings, the irresistible, fast trains enveloped in lights rings of smoke are engulfed in platforms. In others, huge locomotives, immobile and widely scattered, await their moment of departure.'

Part of George Rivière's review of Interior of the Gare St-Lazare 1877

thirty-five

Claude Monet (1840-1926) *Gare St-Lazare*

Pierre August Renoir (1841-1919) *Luncheon of the Boating Party*

'... is a charming work, full of gaiety and spirit, its wild youth caught in the act, radiant and lively, frolicking at high noon in the sun, laughing at everything, seeing only today and mocking tomorrow. For them eternity is in their glass, in their boat, and in their songs. It is fresh and free without being too bawdy.'

Comment of Paul de Charry in *Le Pays* of *The Luncheon of the Boating Party*

Louis Anquetin (1861-1932) *Street Scene, at Five in the Afternoon*

A street there is in Paris famous,
  For which no rhyme our language yields,
  Rue Neuve des Petits Champs its name is —
The New Street of the Little Fields;
And here's an inn, not rich and splendid,
  But still in comfortable case;
The which in youth I oft attended,
  To eat a bowl of Bouillabaisse.

This Bouillabaisse a noble dish is —
  A sort of soup or broth, or brew,
A hotchpotch, of all sorts of fishes,
  That Greenwich never could outdo;
Green herbs, red peppers, mussels, saffern,
  Soles, onions, garlic, roach, and dace;
All these you eat at Terré's tavern,
  In that one dish of Bouillabaisse.

Indeed, a rich and savoury stew 'tis;
  And true philosophers, methinks,
Who love all sorts of natural beauties,
  Should love good victuals and good drinks.
And Cordelier or Benedictine
  Might gladly, sure, his lot embrace,
Nor find a fast-day too afflicting
  Which served him up a Bouillabaisse.

From: *The Ballad of Bouillabaisse*. William Makepeace Thackeray 1811-1863

Edgar Degas (1834-1917) *At the Milliner's*

'His skill as a colourist, and as one who can suggest – we can hardly say who can elaborately paint – texture, is shown in another design, the astonishing picture of two young women trying on bonnets in a milliner's shop. Half of the design is occupied by the milliner's table on which lies a store of her finery. Silks and feathers, satin and straw, are indicated swiftly, decisively, with a most brilliant touch.'

Frederick Wedmore

The cypress stood up like a church
  That night we felt our love would hold,
And saintly moonlight seemed to search
  And wash the whole world clean gold;
The olives crystallised the vales'
  Broad slopes until the hills grew strong:
The fireflies and the nightgales
  Throbbed each to either, flame and song,
The nightingales, the nightingales!

Upon the angle of its shade
  The cypress stood, self-balanced high;
Half up, half down, as double-made,
  Along the ground, against the sky;
And we, too! from such soul-height went
  Such leaps of blood, so blindly driven,
We scarce knew if our nature meant
  More passionate earth or intense heaven.
The nightingales, the nightingales!

From: *Bianca Among the Nightingales*. Elizabeth Barrett Browning 1806-1861

forty-one

Edouard Manet (1832-1883) *Déjeuner sur l'herbe*

'The public were scandalised by this nude, which was all it saw in the painting. "Good heavens! How indecent! A woman without a stitch on alongside two clothed men". Such a thing had never been seen before! But that was a gross mistake, for in the Louvre there are more than fifty canvases in which both clothed and nude figures appear.'

Emile Zola 1840-1902

‘Up to the present,
Degas has known
better than anyone
else how to capture the
spirit of modern life’

Edmond de Goncourt

Edgar Degas (1834-1917) *Breakfast after a Bath*

Hush! my dear, lie still and slumber,
  Holy angels guard thy bed!
Heavenly blessings without number
  Gently falling on thy head.

Sleep, my babe; thy food and raiment,
  House and home, thy friends provide;
All without thy care and payment:
  All thy wants are well supplied.

How much better thou'rt attended
  Than the Son of God could be,
When from heaven He descended
  And became a child like thee.

Isaac Watts 1674-1748

Berthe Morisot (1841-1895) *The Cradle*

Six centuries now have gone

Since, one by one,

These stones were laid,

And in air's vacancy

This beauty made.

They who thus reared them

Their long rest have won;

Ours now this heritage –

To guard, preserve, delight in, brood upon;

And in these transitory fragments scan

The immortal longings in the soul of Man.

Walter de la Mare 1873-1956

Camille Pissarro (1831-1903) *Portal of the Church of St-Jacques, Dieppe*

"I've transformed –
demolished – all my
paintings with sunshine"

Claude Monet